What's *The Writing Notebook*?

You're about to embark on a book about food. Maybe it's a cookbook or a love story, a family memoir, or a research-intensive historical survey of a single ingredient, such as peppercorns or beef or lettuce. Maybe the idea for the book has been simmering for a while, you've been collecting recipes for years, or you've fallen in love and all you want to do is bake. Something has compelled you to start this writing journey.

For now, what matters is writing the book. A book, like any elaborate meal, takes time. Time to get the words onto paper, time to get distracted and come back to the story, time to work out what the story is. You can start with an idea for the book, though by the time you get to the end of the first draft, you'll probably - and hopefully! - discover that your initial plan has changed, you've learnt something new about your characters, about the settings, about the narrative, even about yourself.

A book is a hungry thing. It's our job to feed it; to be open and generous and vulnerable. We have our entire lives to offer up: childhood memories, lovers, family members, friends, jobs, bosses, even our own children! Everything is fodder for the book. If you're reading this, you already have enough material to complete a book. As Flannery O'Connor pointed out, a writer only has to survive their childhood to have sufficient material to last a lifetime. Add to that bank of resources everything you've ever read, overheard, listened to, felt, touched, eaten, cooked, baked, and imagined. The challenge will be to stay open so that everything remains available for the book you're writing, whether it's a novel, a collection of recipes, a non-fiction study, or a family memoir.

Every story is an accumulation of scenes arranged in an order to create suspense, delight and surprise. *The Writing Notebook* is devised to get you to write those scenes in all their variety, their drama and vivid detail. The notebook is set out in a way that allows you to start anywhere, move around, write wherever you are, come back to sections, keep going. You decide on your approach. You can work through the notebook from beginning to end, the first page till the last, or you can move around, revisit sections, write in fragments or come at it as a continuous narrative. You can write in this notebook and continue in another, or on your laptop, take notes on your phone. There is more than one way to write a book. In the process of writing, you'll discover which way works best for you.

The notebook is devised to make it easy for you to incorporate your writing into your everyday life. Have it with you during your lunch-break, in the kitchen while you cook or while you watch someone bake. Use whatever you encounter in the world for a scene in the novel. Nurture your writing practice through focus and stillness. *The Writing Notebook* will not distract you with notifications and pop ups, it won't lure you into checking your Twitter feed or your emails. This is a dedicated space for your writing and for your imagination to play; a place for you. This notebook is both a guide and a journey in itself.

What *The Writing Notebook* is not

Finding out what to do with a completed manuscript is the easy bit. That's not our job here. It can be a lengthy and arduous process to find an agent, an editor, a publisher, then to market the book, talk about it, get press coverage. There are tried and tested ways to do all of this, and if you follow them, eventually something will happen. Or you can self-publish, do your own promotion, set up a series of events. There are dozens of how-to books and vast online resources to guide you through those processes.

The Writing Notebook is a space to write your book, or at least a substantial chunk of it. It's not a guide to writing a cover letter to a publisher, or to finding an agent or to marketing. Here, your book is what matters, and, for now, the focus will be on writing it. Make the writing of your book a meaningful experience. Try to ensure that you have said everything you can say and want to say about this story and that you have created a unique world, done everything you can to make it the book it wants to be.

What do I need in order to write a book?

You'll need content, some research, a desire to write a book, experience and community. Writing a book takes commitment and ritual and enquiry - it requires a sense of curiosity to unearth something, but also a compulsion to tell a story. A book is also a way of saying "I was here, this is my offering." You have to want to write a book to write a book. There's a proverb that says that if you want to go fast, go it alone; to go far - go together. Writing a book is the long haul! Find people to write with, whether it's a writing buddy you meet up with, or an online forum. Ask a friend to check in with you, to send you a text or email reminding you to write. Explore what works for you and find someone to be part of this journey. Make the process exist in the world even before you've finished the book. If you'd rather rely on books, find the right books to keep you company while you work your way towards creating your own. *The Writing Notebook* will do its best to be good company, to prompt you and send you off in new directions, and will try to make sure you'll want to keep writing.

What's in *The Writing Notebook*?

The Writing Notebook will provide you with writing suggestions, guidance and space to write your next book. This is where you'll be able to think about your book; to put into words the context, the ideas and the rationale behind the creation of your book, as well as the questions, passion and urgency that make you want to sit down and excavate this story.

The Writing Notebook will get you to focus on all aspects of food and how it relates to place, ways of preparation, time, and to the ways we live our lives. It will help you create a rich and layered narrative. *The Writing Notebook* will prompt you to move gradually and dramatically through the story you're writing, the cookbook you're compiling, or the book you're researching. You are welcome to adapt the exercises and writing ideas to suit your book, and play with the illustrations - add to them, colour them in - and draw new ones. Throughout the notebook I've tried to keep the prompts brief, yet also specific and comprehensive, to offer suggestions and then get out of your way, so that you can make the notebook your own.

Description workouts

Some sections in *The Writing Notebook* invite you to focus on description. These workouts, whether to describe a location, a person or an ingredient, will deepen your understanding of the world you're creating. Through description, you make the world of your book real. You are the creator; it's up to you to know exactly what that world looks like and feels like. Description situates you firmly in the world of your book, and because of that, will engage your readers' imagination on a visceral level. "Good description is a learned skill," says Stephen King in his book, *On Writing*. "Reading will help you answer how much, and only reams of writing will help you with the how."

Gathering

Stories are everywhere to be gathered and incorporated into your bank of resources. These writing activities will prompt you to tackle things you may not have done before, experiment with new ways of finding stories, add new tricks to your repertoire, and try out new ingredients. These exercises may become new stories or projects, or, with minor adjustments, will blend into your book. Every story you imagine, every experience you have, and every skill you acquire adds to the range of your writing, offering you ideas for this project and for others that will grow out of the book you're writing now.

Use these first few sections to jot down notes and keep adding to them as you progress through the notebook. Here you'll explore the themes of your book, who it might appeal to, its concerns, settings and chronology. Many of these elements will become clearer to you as you complete this first draft. Think of these first few pages as a space for exploring possibilities and options.

Write down what your book is about. Think in practical terms. For instance "This is a book about a cook who lives on a remote island…" or: "This is a book about the role of festive meals in a family…" or: "A book about a woman who opens a chocolate shop across the road from the priest's house." Think about the abstract themes of the book. It might be about co-existence, love, betrayal, or a collection of ingredients, people, or countries. It might be about survival (of dishes or people), or about creativity. It could "simply" be a book about pies or about cod. For now, maybe you'll only have a few ideas; more will come as you work your way through the book.

Start with the phrase "This is a book about…" and keep coming back to it as you write.

Write about the different audiences you want your book to appeal to. You'll keep coming back to this list as you work your way through the book. Yes, it's a book about food, but it may also appeal, similar to *Like Water for Chocolate*, to readers interested in Mexican history, or magic realism, or a good love story. Launch yourself into the next few pages with a phrase: "This book is for people who..." If, for example, you're writing a book with oyster recipes and you want marine biologists to read it, what could you add to the book to appeal to them? As you write, explore how different audiences inspire new themes and recipes for your book. Write about audiences you may not initially have thought about, or ask others to suggest who your book could appeal to. Then, make notes about possible scenes and chapters you could add to your book. Write the book you want to write, but also keep looking for ways to make it a rewarding and surprising adventure for yourself.

Write about some of the big questions you're tackling in the book. Questions about love, sustainability, obsession, right and wrong, immigration, famine. Write down the more manageable questions, too, such as, how to make the perfect paella, or the secrets of foraging, or who in your family makes the best Christmas pudding. Use some of these questions to explore who else has written about similar subjects, and the ways in which your book is or could be different. These questions will increase your awareness of the book's purpose and your compulsion to write it.

The notes in these sections can lay the groundwork for your book's introduction, its preface, foreword or afterword. List some thoughts now, and keep returning to these pages.

This is the place to think about how you'd like to organise your book. You could order it in terms of months, ingredients, or seasons. You could create a story through flashbacks. Think about dividing your book up into different sections and chapters. Think about movement and variety. Don't let your book be static. If you organise your book according to the seasons, you'll create a sense of movement through time and also provide yourself with a natural structure. Organising it by city or country will allow you to move through space. Explore how others have structured their books about food and make a note of various options. You could start in January and end in December, or arrange your book by menus or meals. See which of these structures works for you, and create new structures of your own.

Explore the tables of contents in various books about food. As you write your book, create a table of contents that delights you. *The Alice B. Toklas Cookbook* includes items such as "Dishes for Artists" and "Murder in the Kitchen" and Yotam Ottolenghi's *Plenty* covers "The Mighty Aubergine" and "Leaves Cooked and Raw". In the table of contents of MFK Fisher's *Consider the Oyster* you'll find "R is for Oyster" and "Pearls Are Not Good to Eat." Even if you decide not to include a table of contents, these pages will give you an overview of your book, and make it easier to spot where the gaps and repetitions are.

Imagine the table of contents as a real table, as vast as you want, with all the richness a list of contents can offer, dishes ready to be eaten. In a book about food, perhaps more than for any other book, a table of contents is an enticing menu, an invitation to a feast.

Write about the preparation of food. Write this in prose or in recipe form. Don't worry about order or chronology; the important thing is to get as many scenes or recipes onto the page. More will come to you as you write. Begin with something simple, a single ingredient, such as an orange; the first story, scene, memory, recipe or historical record of oranges. Or aubergines, rice, red peppers, chocolate, carp. Write in a way that interests you and that emerges from your own life, even if you're writing fiction.

Write scenes or recipes that involve different ways of preparing food: frying, baking, drying, grilling, preserving, barbecuing, steaming, stir-frying, or eating food raw. You could write about different types of food being prepared, or pick a single ingredient and show what happens when your character fries, bakes, preserves, or eats it raw. Especially if you have one main character in the book - even if that character is you - experiment with ways of creating variety and movement. One scene or recipe might be based on a memory, the other on a story passed down, and another inspired by research.

.

In writing your story or compiling your recipes, become aware of contrasts, seasons and times of day. Notice interesting clashes in colour, different ways of sourcing food and the different places food comes from. Create dynamism in the range of recipes and in the actions involved in sourcing ingredients. Write about an ingredient that's particularly difficult to find, and the story of how it has been sourced over the centuries. Or write about a dish that's exceptionally challenging to make. Write about food "then and now": a meal that was eaten in the character's past, or your past, or the ancestral past, and a dish that is eaten in the present. Let your recipes and your ingredients clash. You could start by listing the types of contrasts relevant to your book.

Write three scenes of conflict:
1) between two characters, 2) between a character and the world or nature, and 3) an internal conflict. Repeat as needed.

Write in detail about a location that is central to your book. This could be a kitchen, a room in a house, a garden, a market, a field, anywhere. It could be somewhere relevant to the story's present or a place that is remembered. Be specific and expansive in your description. Do research, if necessary. Imagine a camera filming what you describe: zoom in, pan out. Write about textures and smells, about sounds heard close by and in the distance, and about colours and taste. Stay focused on the description, on what the senses experience. If you drift into story or psychology, bring yourself back to the act of describing. Write more than you'll need. It's easier to delete than to expand during the rewriting stage. Strengthen your observing muscles to the point where describing is a joy. Repeat whenever at a loss for something to write. Description will bring you back into the story.

Go shopping for food. Use the experience of shopping to feed into your story. Buy something for your character as a gift, or shop as your character would shop; purchase the ingredients they'll need for a dish. Take notes as you shop, and stop at regular intervals to write a few paragraphs. Make a plan before you set out. Limit yourself to three different shops or only buy what you need for a single meal. Speak to people, gather information, imagine the lives of those you encounter and how you might use these details for your book. Be open to the unexpected and the layers it can add to your book.

Explore several timeframes that could contain your story. Food is closely linked to time: sell-by dates; the time it takes to prepare a meal; the time it takes to eat a meal; the time it takes to grow ingredients; or the age at which an animal is ready to be eaten. The time-frame could be from winter to autumn, from infatuation to marriage, from the beginning of a fast to the end of it, or from morning coffee to nightcap. Revisit the notes you made on page 23.

Write three scenes or recipes from very different points along your timeframe. The first scene could be something to do with beginnings: planting, falling in love, or a discovery. The second scene could have something to do with middles, peaks, or a dish that is moderately difficult to prepare. The last scene could include an extremely complex meal, the end of a love affair, or a triumph. These scenes don't necessarily have to appear in this order in the final book, but they will ensure that you have variety and movement. Cast the net of your story wide.

Write about the central images in your book. If you're creating a recipe book, make sketches or take photos, print out or cut out pictures to paste here. Create a mood board. Keep a record of the images you want in your book even if you don't plan to include drawings or photographs. If you're writing fiction or a memoir, write in detail about these images, translate them into prose. Often, these are the images that will stay in your mind - and the reader's mind - long after you've finished writing the book. Take your time. Include a variety of images: pictures of single ingredients, places where food is made, close ups and panoramic views, bird's-eye views, photos of machinery and cooking utensils, people cooking, baking, eating and washing up (see also the strawberry exercise on page 131).

Writing about food gives you license to write about how we live our lives. Comment, judge, categorise, generalise, and make bold statements about people, about love, about dying, about eating, about family, and whatever feels relevant to your book. You are the author and you have the authority. Own it. In just one small book, *Consider the Oyster*, MFK Fisher starts almost every chapter with a bold proclamation, the kind of statement that makes you want to find out more. Her opening lines include: "There are three kinds of oyster-eaters..." and "The flavor of an oyster depends on several things..." and "There are several things to do with oysters beside eat them..."

Try out some examples using the same sentence structure, a similar kind of assertive beginning. "There are several things to do with [aubergines/lovers/chocolate/insert item of your choice] besides..." or "There are three kinds of [you choose!]..." This is where you write down *your* thoughts on the food, the characters and the ideas in your book. Allow yourself to be wise and expansive and forthright. You could write this as a scene with dialogue, or get your characters to make those bold statements for you.

Try to bring as much of the world as you can into your book. Write about 1) food that is grown or lives on the land, 2) food that lives in the sea, and 3) food that comes from the air. Write three separate scenes: one that shows food and the soil or underground, another that tells a story about food and the sea, and a third that links food and sky. Think broadly. For example, write about a meal on land, a meal on a cruise ship, and a meal on a plane flying over the Atlantic. Bring movement into your book. Notice where your focus lingers, and then, after a while, shift it.

See if there's a way to join two or more of the scenes together. Find ways to transition from land to water, or from air to sea, the way a bird swoops down to pluck a fish from the ocean. Everything we eat and everything we grow - everything that lives! - relies on land, water and air. Create scenes in which your characters engage with all these elements. Include recipes based primarily in those distinct "realms" and others that bring them together, such as underground with underwater, carrots and calamari.

Go for a walk with your notebook. In your neighbourhood, or your favourite part of town, or in another city. Make notes or brief sketches about what you imagine people are eating in the houses and buildings you pass. Write about food served in the restaurants and cafés on your way. This walk could also be from memory, or an amalgam of imaginary walks. Alternatively, let your character do the walking for you. If you're writing a cookbook, you could punctuate the walk with recipes, and stop off at places to taste and try out new dishes. Not everything we write has to be immediately linked to The Book. It's important to step out of the plan and write for fun; later on, you can consider how or if you want to fit this into the main project. You can also add some of these ideas to your future projects list on page 155.

Read through what you've written about your walk. Join some of the fragments together. Find ways to tweak and expand what you've written to fit into your book. A book is written at a specific point in time; everything we write during that time is created out of the same state of our imagination. Everything fits.

Write about a meal that you or your character are preparing. As you write the story of the present, move back and forth in time. Let different actions and ingredients trigger memories or other recipes, let the mind wonder into the future, imagine what will happen when the food is served. Write about expectations and reminiscences, all the while keeping your eye on the cake being baked, or the stew being prepared. Let the duration of the meal - the preparation, the eating, the clearing up - frame this chapter.

You could go back to the source of the main ingredient, right back to the seed, if it's a plant, or to the birth, if it's a creature. A good example of this is Rachel Carson's book *Under the Sea-Wind*. Start from the earliest point in the life cycle, then go all the way forward to what happens to left overs that get recycled or washed out to sea. This movement back and forth in time will generate new ideas, and you might want to break up this section into several stories. With writing, as with all things that grow, the unexpected can - and hopefully *does* - happen. When you start planting, or cooking, or writing you can't know where you'll land up.

2.

3.

4.

5.

6.

Write a detailed description of a character. Write it in prose and as part of a scene. Maybe they're looking at themselves in a mirror or at their reflection in a silver bowl, maybe they're being observed by someone else. Write about their features, their hair, how they move, what they wear, and the details of their hands, chest, legs, feet. You can always edit things out afterwards. Use this workout to gain intimate knowledge of your characters. Repeat as necessary.

If you want to continue on from the previous few pages, this could be the scene after the meal when everyone has left and you or your character are alone. Cookbooks need characters, too. Describe some of the people responsible for your recipes.

What are you up against? Who or what is getting in the way? Write about those characters obstructing your main character, or bigger disruptive forces such as war and famine. Write about what or who is making the sharing of food a challenge. Create three scenes from different points in the story in which your character is trying to give food or get to food and someone or something is stopping them. Show us the scene. Be the camera. Stories rely on drama. Be clear as to what your character wants, then find ways to make it difficult for them.

Cookbooks, too, need drama and conflict. Elizabeth David writes about post-war rationing and scarcity in her collection of rich and abundant recipes, *A Book of Mediterranean Food*.

Stay with conflict and challenges for a while longer. Write two scenes that show the opposite of what you've been writing about. If a character has a sweet tooth, create a character who only eats savoury dishes. Write about recipes that flopped and were fixed, or a scene where your character has to deal with the aftermath of a meal ruined. Write about not eating, whether out of choice or through being denied food. Write about fasting. These themes will add new layers to your story. They might be anecdotes told to your characters, or stories that exist in the family. Think about different relationships to food - gorging, starving, denying, relishing - and then create two scenes showing very different attitudes to eating or serving food.

Pause to take stock. Write about how you got to this point. What lies behind you writing this book, your motivation for researching this subject, or collecting these recipes? If you want to focus on your character, tell the story of how their passion for food evolved, or what has compelled them to do what they do. Write about the role of cooking and baking in your life and in the life of your character.

Explore your connection to this story and where you stand in relation to its subject matter. If it's a recipe book, what do these recipes and ingredients mean to you? If it's non-fiction, how does your own story fit into the bigger story? Revisit what you wrote on page 17.

Write three different scenes in which your character is eating a meal. In the first scene they are alone; in the second - with one other person; and in the third scene they're with a large group of friends, family, colleagues, or strangers. Think about bringing variety to the types of meals and types of relationships in your book. In one scene, you could have food that heals: chicken soup, lemon and ginger, turmeric. In another scene, food could feature as the cause of harm, whether through allergy, poisoning or being rotten. Food could be used to tempt or seduce. Or alternatively, to destroy or repel. Sketch the layout of the table and note where your characters are sitting. There can be drama in the way bodies are situated in relation to each other. If you're writing a cookbook, write about remedies; about food that heals and increases pleasure. You could also give warnings about certain foods, about what happens when it goes off, or risky combinations of ingredients. Explore recipes that inspire a spectrum of reactions.

Take a strawberry by its stalk and place it on a piece of paper. This is a description workout in several stages. 1) Write about what you can see. Just the details of what is there before you. Don't touch the strawberry. Translate what you see into words. No story, just description. Force yourself to spend at least 7 minutes on each section. 2) Pick up the strawberry and write about smell and touch. Put it against your cheek or against your skin. But don't let it brush against your lips. Focus on scent and texture. 3) Write about what you *think* the strawberry will taste like and feel like in your mouth. Write about your expectation. 4) End with a story, memory or scene from your book that involves strawberries. Explore the potential of a single ingredient. Notice how a story emerges from close observation. Repeat as desired. Whenever you feel blocked, detailed and careful description will bring you back into your work.

Fiction is the slow and meticulous transcribing of the imagined, the feared, and the desired. Write about what you don't know: food you've never eaten, meals you've never prepared, pastries you've never baked. Use the energy of curiosity and not-knowing to fuel your imagination. This could be a dream, or a character preparing a dish you've never made. Write in detail. Pretend you know.

Alternatively, learn something new. Sign up to a course or get someone to teach you to make their favourite dish. Observe. Record stories. Courses and workshops give you access to new stories. Write down your experience in as much detail as you can. Use this experience of something new as a way to gain insight into your character and how they've learnt to cook and bake. If you're writing a memoir, create two scenes in which knowledge is being imparted, whether through demonstration or through conversation.

Write the ending of your story. Sometimes it helps to write the end before you reach it; that way you can relax into the telling of the story. Be open to changing the ending by the time you actually get to it. Revisit your notes about the organisation of the book on page 23 and your thoughts on the timeframe on page 59. If the book starts in summer, does it end in winter, or maybe the beginning of the following summer? If you've organised it according to the days of the week, what would be the best day to end it on? Write two or three different endings. Think about the image that you want to linger at the end of the book. Think about what happens at the end of a meal, and how that could inform your ending. A messy table, satisfied guests, quarrelling hosts, people walking home, early morning, midnight, arrival at a restaurant after hours of driving through the hills. Consider the predictable ending, and then create a final scene to surprise your reader and yourself.

This might be the first book of its kind that your reader encounters. If you're writing a cookbook, share your tips on preparing, freezing, best places and how to shop. Write about how you'd like your readers to approach the book and what you'd like them to get out of it. You're bringing something unique to the table - write about it, even if you feel it's been written about before. If you're writing fiction or a memoir, incorporate some of your knowledge about sourcing and preparing food into three different scenes. Your way of making chocolate brownies, your way of growing tomatoes, your way of boiling an egg. Build stories around your methods and techniques. Think about expanding or reducing the world of your book. Set these scenes in different countries and different landscapes, or confine all the action to one tiny kitchen.

Make a note of whom you want to thank. And places, too. It's a way of reminding yourself who, where and what helped you complete the writing of your book. Be as quirky as you like. Thank your favourite butcher, your grandmother for her fudge, or the barista at your local coffee shop. Thank other writers.

Write down some future projects you'd like to work on. Books you want to tackle or smaller projects you could rustle up in a day or two: flash fiction, blog posts, articles. Avoid being distracted while working on your current project, though make sure you have new ideas for when you're done or need a breather from The Book.

21 Books you might like to read

Diana Abu-Jaber. *The Language of Baklava.*
Steve Almond. *Candyfreak.*
Karen Blixen. *Babette's Feast.*
Aldo Buzzi. *The Perfect Egg and Other Secrets.*
Lewis Carroll. *Alice's Adventures in Wonderland.*
Roald Dahl. *Charlie and the Chocolate Factory.*
Elizabeth David. *A Book of Mediterranean Food.*
Janet Frame. *Towards Another Summer.*
Laura Esquivel. *Like Water for Chocolate.*
MFK Fisher. *Consider the Oyster.*
Joanne Harris. *Chocolat.*
Molly Katzen. *Still Life with Menu Cookbook.*
Mark Kurlansky. *Cod.*
Torgny Lindgren. *Sweetness.*
Amelie Nothomb. *The Life of Hunger.*
Yotam Ottolenghi. *Plenty.*
Colette Rossant. *Apricots on the Nile.*
Maurice Sendak. *In the Night Kitchen.*
David E. Sutton. *Remembrance of Repasts.*
Alice B. Toklas. *The Alice B. Toklas Cookbook.*
Anne Tyler. *Dinner at the Homesick Restaurant.*

List of Prompts

What's your book about?	9
Who's the book for?	13
The big questions	17
Organising your book	23
Your table of contents	27
Preparing and ways of making	31
Contrast and conflict	39
The places of food	47
Go shopping	53
The timeframe	59
Images that linger	65
Making grand statements	73
Land, sea, and air	77
Taking food for a walk	85
From seed to sea, back and forth	91
The people of your book	97
Who's getting in the way	103
Food flops and famine	111
Taking stock	117
Food that harms and food that heals	123
Consider the strawberry	131
Learn something new	135
Who does the washing up?	143
Your tips	149
Acknowledgements	153
Future projects	155
21 books you might like to read	157

BIS Publishers
Building Het Sieraad
Postjesweg 1
1057 DT Amsterdam
The Netherlands
T +31 (0)20 515 02 30
F +31 (0)20 515 02 39
bis@bispublishers.nl
www.bispublishers.nl

Written and devised by Shaun Levin
Designed by Beldan Sezen
Illustrations and cover design by Andrew Carter

ISBN 978 90 6369 392 3